The Potato Cookbook

THE POTATO COOKBOOK

GWEN McIVER

B T Batsford Ltd, London

*Line drawings by
Brenda Naylor*

*Jacket drawing and those facing title
page and on pages 8 and 87 by
Judith Hamp*

© Gwen McIver
First Published 1977
ISBN 0 7134 0477 9

Made and printed in Great Britain by
The Anchor Press Ltd, Tiptree, Essex
Phototypeset by Trident Graphics Ltd
Reigate, Surrey
for the publishers
B T Batsford Ltd
4 Fitzhardinge Street, London W1H 0AH

Contents

Miscellaneous Potato Recipes

Introduction

The potato, as far as is known, came from South America, more specifically from the higher altitudes of Peru, Bolivia and southern Chile. It was found by Spaniards invading South America before 1492. The American Indians called it *pappas*.

It is believed that Spanish sailors introduced potatoes into Spain and Portugal in the 1560s, where they were then known as *batatas* or *batates*. From there they were taken to Italy and thence to Holland, Germany, Switzerland and finally to France in the early seventeenth century. The potato was first grown experimentally in England in 1586 and soon spread to Ireland. It was probably introduced from Spain, although there is a legend that Sir Francis Drake brought it on a voyage from the West Indies in 1586. However, potatoes did not really become popular in England until about 1900.

There are many things that can be done with the potato, apart from baking, roasting, boiling, chipping, mashing, croquetting, creaming, scalloping, or making into a casserole. There are cups, baskets, dumplings, salads, omelettes, pancakes, etc, so never think of the potato as an ordinary or lowly vegetable. There are over a hundred different varieties of which the red *King Edward* or the *Golden Wonder* are said to be the favourites, although the *Aura*, the *Kerebel* and the *Portland Crown* are best for chips or potato salad. The *Fir Apple* is also very good, but I must admit that I use all types, especially new potatoes when they are in season.

When cooking potatoes, always cook them in their jackets if possible, as they retain more goodness that way. The potato contains a small amount of vitamin C and a good deal of protein.

I have lived in many countries because of my husband's work, and half the time I had no idea of what type of potato I was cooking, but I always seemed to have success. One of the main things to remember when boiling potatoes is not to overcook them to let them become mushy. I sometimes lift out some of the smaller ones and let the large ones cook a little longer. I find that experimenting with cooking potatoes is half the fun and I hope that after you try out some of my recipes you will agree.

It is easier now that the markets offer 'instant' packet potatoes which can be used for mash, croquette, or dumpling recipes. There are also many gadgets now in use such as the potato chipper, the spike potato baker, as well as potato mashers, ricers, and ball makers, and of course the good old potato peeler.

Boiled Potatoes

Boiled Potatoes

Boiled potatoes should always be cooked with skins if possible. If peeled, the smallest amount of skin should be removed.

Boiled New Potatoes

Scrub small new potatoes with soft brush, put into boiling salted water and cook for 25 minutes. Serve in their skins, with butter.

Cheese Potatoes

8 hot boiled potatoes
½ cup grated cheese
¼ cup melted butter
Salt and pepper, to taste

Roll hot potatoes in melted butter, then in cheese mixed with salt and pepper. Place in a baking tin and bake in 400° or no. 6 oven for 15 minutes.

serves 8

Browned Potatoes

8 medium potatoes
2 tablespoons butter
2 tablespoons flour
¼ pint stock
1 medium chopped onion
1 small chopped sour
   gherkin
1 oz raisins
1 oz currants
Salt and pepper, to taste

Boil potatoes and peel, keep warm. Fry butter until just brown, add flour and mix with butter; gradually add stock, then salt and pepper, onion, gherkin, raisins and currants and cook for 2 minutes. Slice the potatoes and add them to the sauce, leaving them until they have absorbed all the sauce and become quite brown. Serve the potatoes with the onion, gherkin, raisins and currants.

serves 6–8

Spanish Boiled Garlic Potatoes

8 medium potatoes
2 dried red peppers
3 cloves garlic
½ teaspoons vinegar
2 teaspoons oil
Paprika and salt

Peel the potatoes and boil with the peppers, drain and slice about ½-inch thick. Crush garlic and mix with paprika, salt, oil and vinegar. Mix gently with sliced potatoes and reheat before sewing.

serves 6–8

Boiled Potatoes with Ham and Tomatoes

4 large boiled potatoes
4 thick slices ham, cut in
half
2 tomatoes
Melted butter
Mustard
Celery salt
Salt and pepper to taste

Peel and cut potatoes in half, lengthwise, and place in buttered casserole dish; brush with melted butter. Spread sliced ham with mustard and place mustard-side down on each potato then a thick slice of tomato on top of each piece, sprinkle with salt, pepper and celery salt. Put in 350° or no. 4 oven for 20 minutes.

serves 4–6

French Potato Balls

24 small new potatoes or
potatoes cut into balls
2 tablespoons butter
3 tablespoons chopped
parsley

If new small potatoes, cook in skin and peel after cooking. If other potatoes are used, peel and cut into balls with potato baller, wash, and cook covered in boiling water for 15 minutes. Drain.

Melt butter in pan, toss parsley in butter, then toss gently potatoes.

serves 5–6

Potatoes in Bechamel Sauce

1 lb potatoes
1½ tablespoons butter
(melted)
3 tablespoons Parmesan
cheese
1½ cups Bechamel sauce

Boil potatoes in skins for 30 minutes, drain and peel, slice in ½-inch slices and mix into Bechamel sauce (see below). Pour the melted butter into casserole dish, sprinkle with 1 tablespoon of Parmesan cheese, add potatoes in sauce and sprinkle with rest of cheese.

serves 4

Bechamel sauce
2 tablespoons butter
1½ tablespoons flour
¼ pint stock
½ pint milk

Melt butter, add flour and mix to smooth paste; add stock gradually, stirring all the time, add milk and keep stirring all the time over heat until thickened.

Steamed Potatoes

Peel and wash potatoes, cut in halves and add for the last 30 minutes to pot roast or stews.

These potatoes always make a pot roast or stew go further.

Boiled Potatoes with Onion

8 medium potatoes
2 medium onions
3 tablespoons butter
Salt and pepper to taste

Peel and wash potatoes, peel and slice onions, put both together in boiling salted water, boil for 30 minutes, drain. Melt butter in saucepan, return potatoes and onions and shake well in butter.

serves 6

Potatoes in Sauce

6 medium potatoes
2 tablespoons butter
2 teaspoons chopped
   parsley
1 onion chopped
1 small green pepper
   chopped
1 cup gravy
Salt and pepper to taste

Wash and boil potatoes for 30 minutes, drain, peel and slice into ½-inch slices.

Melt butter in pan, fry onions, add green peppers and parsley, add sliced potatoes, salt and pepper, then add gravy and mix altogether gently over heat. Cover and simmer for few minutes.

serves 4

Pomme Maitre D'Hotel

8 medium potatoes
¼ teaspoon salt
½ teaspoon paprika
¼ cup melted butter
2 tablespoons chopped
   parsley
1 tablespoon lemon juice

Wash and cook potatoes in skins, boil for 30 minutes, drain, peel. To melted butter add parsley, salt, paprika and lemon juice; then add potatoes, and turn carefully coating them all over with mixture. Serve very hot.

serves 4—6

German Brown Potatoes

6 large potatoes
½ cabbage, finely
   shredded
2 tablespoons dripping
1 tablespoon minced
   onion
½ pint red wine
1 teaspoon brown sugar
Salt and pepper to taste

Wash and boil potatoes, about 20 minutes, drain and peel and cut in half.

Melt fat, fry onion and cabbage for 5 minutes, add brown sugar, red wine, salt and pepper; mix potatoes with cabbage and cook until wine has disappeared, about 20 minutes. Watch that cabbage does not burn on bottom of pan, stir gently once or twice.

serves 6

New Potatoes and Caraway Seeds

2 lb small new potatoes
4 tablespoons butter
Freshly ground pepper
1 teaspoon caraway seeds
Salt to taste

Boil potatoes in skins until cooked. When cool enough to handle, peel. Heat butter in frying pan, add potatoes, sprinkle with salt, caraway seeds and pepper. Cover pan and heat thoroughly but make sure there is no burning. Put into serving dish.

serves 6–8

Mashed Potatoes

Mashed Potatoes

6 potatoes
2 tablespoons butter
½ cup (evaporated) milk
Salt and pepper to taste

Wash and boil potatoes in their skins for 30 minutes, drain. Peel and mash with potato masher (or fork) with butter, salt and pepper. When well mashed, add milk gradually until potatoes are creamy and fluffy. Reheat stirring over stove.

serves 4–6

Riced Potatoes

1 lb potatoes
Salt and paprika

Peel and wash potatoes and boil for 30 minutes. Drain and force through potato ricer or coarse strainer. Sprinkle with salt and paprika, serve with butter.

serves 4–6

Almond Potatoes

2 cups mashed potatoes
2 tablespoons grated
  cheese
2 eggs
Fat for frying
3 tablespoons shredded
  almonds
Salt and cayenne
  pepper
3 tablespoons butter

Mix potatoes, cheese, salt and sprinkle of cayenne together and mix with 1 beaten egg. Roll into small balls and dip into the other beaten egg then roll in almonds until well coated. Drop into hot fat until golden brown and drain on absorbent paper.

serves 6

Chantilly Potatoes

2 cups mashed potatoes
¼ cup cream
¼ cup grated cheese
Salt and paprika

Place the mashed potatoes in a greased casserole dish. Whip cream, add cheese, salt and paprika and pour over mashed potato. Cook in 350° or no. 4 oven for 30 minutes.

serves 6

Mashed Potato with Onion or Chives

3 cups hot mashed
  potatoes
½ cup milk
½ cup finely chopped
  onion or
  3 tablespoons chives
  chopped fine
3 tablespoons butter
Salt and pepper to taste

Mash butter with potatoes and salt and pepper; add milk gradually, then stir in onion or chives and mix well.

serves 8

Potato Cases

4 cups mashed potatoes
¼ cup evaporated milk
2 tablespoons butter
Melted butter
2 eggs (beaten)
Salt and pepper to taste

Mash the 3 tablespoons butter with mashed potatoes, add salt, pepper, milk and egg and blend all well together. Take a ball of potato, about 2½ inches in diameter, push down the centre and push up the sides to form a cup. There should be ½-inch thickness on the bottom and cases should be about 1½ inches high. Brush with melted butter and place on greased baking sheet in 350° or no. 4 oven until golden brown—about 15 to 20 minutes.

These cases can be filled with vegetables or creamed chicken or mushrooms. They can be pinched together at each end and called Potato Boats.

serves 8

Potato Volcano with Cheese

3 cups of prepared
  mashed potato
½ cup grated cheese
1 egg (beaten)
¼ cup butter
Breadcrumbs
Salt and paprika

Put the potatoes on a greased baking sheet, make a circle and hollow in the middle, building it up at the sides about 3 inches high, about 5 inches wide at top of hollow and 1 inch of potato at bottom.

Melt butter, add grated cheese, salt and paprika and egg, beat well together and pour into hollow, bringing some up the inside. Brush the inside with melted butter and sprinkle all with breadcrumbs. Bake in 350° or no. 4 oven for 20 minutes or until golden brown.

serves 6

Potato Drops

2 cups mashed potato
2 eggs, well beaten
Salt and pepper to taste
Fat for frying

Mix the mashed potato with eggs, salt and pepper and beat all well. Drop a spoonful of this mixture into very hot fat—if spoon is dipped into boiling water after each drop, they will drop off the spoon in perfect shape. Fry until golden drown and drain on absorbent paper.

serves 4

Potato Stuffing

3 cups hot mashed potato
1 onion, chopped
¼ cup chopped celery
¼ cup evaporated milk
½ cup pork sausage meat
½ cup breadcrumbs
1 egg, well beaten
½ teaspoon mustard
Salt and paprika to taste

Mix all ingredients very well with hot mashed potato. This is delicious in chicken or a crown roast. If there is any over, depending on size of chicken or roast, cook in small buttered casserole dish in moderate oven for 25 minutes.

Potato Pears

3 cups mashed potato
½ cup evaporated milk
1 egg yolk beaten with
   2 teaspoons water
½ cup grated cheese
6 cloves and paprika
Salt and pepper to taste

To the mashed potato add milk, cheese, salt and pepper and mash well together; divide into 6 equal parts, roll out each piece into the shape of a pear, brush with egg yolk, sprinkle paprika on one side of pear and put the ball part of clove at the bottom and stem end at top, lift them onto a greased tim. Heat in 350° or no. 4 oven for 20 minutes.

serves 6

Eggs in Potato Blankets

3 cups mashed potato
1 egg beaten plus
   2 tablespoons water
4 hard boiled eggs
Breadcrumbs
Fat for frying

Divide the mashed potato into 4 equal parts and shape evenly around each hard-boiled egg, dip into egg mixture and then breadcrumbs and drop into hot fat; cook until golden brown. Drain on absorbent paper, cut in half and serve with tomato sauce.

serves 4

Duchess Potatoes

Cadbury Smash or
   Wonder Mash can be used
2 cups hot mashed
   potatoes
2 tablespoon butter
½ teaspoon salt
2 eggs, separated

Combine mashed potatoes with butter, salt and
beaten egg yolk, shape into balls and put into
buttered casserole dish; brush with slightly beaten
egg whites. Brown in 425°F or no. 7 oven for 15
minutes.

serves 6

Pomme De Terre Duchesse

2 cups mashed potatoes
2 tablespoons butter
Pinch of nutmeg
2 eggs plus 2 egg yolks,
   beaten together
Salt and pepper

Add butter, salt and pepper, nutmeg and beaten
eggs to mashed potatoes and beat with wooden
spoon until light and fluffy. Make little patties about
¼-inch thick and fry in hot butter until brown on
both sides.

serves 6

Mashed Potatoes Au Gratin

6 potatoes, riced
3 tablespoons butter
¼ cup grated Cheddar
   cheese
2 eggs, well beaten
½ teaspoon paprika
½ teaspoon salt
½ cup breadcrumbs

Put cooked potatoes through ricer or force through
coarse strainer; add butter, paprika, salt and eggs to
riced potatoes; put into greased baking pan and
cover with cheese and breadcrumbs. Cook in 375° on
no. 5 oven for 20 minutes until breadcrumbs are
brown.

serves 4

Potato Puff Balls

You can use *Cadbury
   Smash* or *Wonder Mash*
   or fresh potatoes for this
   recipe
2 cups warm mashed
   potatoes
2 eggs, separated
1 tablespoon chopped
   parsley
1 teaspoon minced onion

Beat potatoes, egg yolks, parsley and onions
together, beat egg whites until stiff and fold into
mixture. Drop a tablespoon full at a time onto
greased baking tin, leaving about 1 inch space
between each. Cook in 350° or no. 4 oven for 30 to 40
minutes, or until golden brown.

serves 6

Pommes Mousseline

2 cups mashed potatoes
2 tablespoons butter
2 teaspoons chopped
   chives
¾ cup milk
2 teaspoons chopped
   watercress
Pepper and salt

Add all ingredients to mashed potatoes and cream to smoothe paste. Heat thoroughly over stove.

serves 6

Baked Potatoes

Baked Potatoes

Always make sure the potatoes are well scrubbed and dried; scrubbing with small brush under running water is a good idea. Also use large potatoes and either prick four or five times with a fork or cut shallow ½-inch cross lengthwise of the potato to let steam out. Allow 1 potato per person.

Baked Jacket Potato

After preparation as above, bake in 425° or no. 7 oven for 45 minutes or until soft. You can tell when cooked if potato is soft when pressed between fingers.

Pomme De Terre Farcies

6 large potatoes
¼ lb sausage meat
1 oz butter or margarine
1 tablespoon finely
   chopped onion
1 tablespoon chopped
   parsley
Salt and pepper

Peel and cut potatoes lengthwise; scoop out large hole in each half and boil scooped-out pieces in salt water until tender, then mash with butter, add sausage meat, onion, parsley, salt and peper and fill holes in raw potatoes. Place in greased casserole dish and bake in 350° or no. 4 oven for 1 hour.

serves 6

Potato Salmon Souffle

6 large potatoes
2 tablespoons butter
3 eggs, beaten
1 tablespoon minced
   piménto
1 teaspoon minced onion
½ cup milk
1 cup flaked salmon
Pepper and salt

Bake the potatoes, cut in half lengthwise and scoop out insides, making sure not to pierce the shells. Mash with butter, add milk, pepper and salt, then onion, piménto and salmon; then add beaten eggs and pile back into potato shells; place in oven and bake for 20 minutes in 350° or no. 4 oven.

serves 6

Baked Potatoes Au Gratin

6 large potatoes
½ lb grated Cheddar
  cheese

Scrub potatoes until very clean and dry well. Cut a large piece out of potato lengthwise 2 inches long, 1 inch wide and 1½ inches deep. Cut all potato of cut-out piece away, leaving the piece ¼-inch thick. Stuff the hole with grated cheese and put cut away potato piece back on top. Cook in a 350° or no. 4 oven for about 1 hour, or until soft.

serves 6

Armenian Potatoes

4 large potatoes
1 tablespoon butter
1 tomato chopped fine
2 cloves garlic, crushed
¼ cup milk
1 small teaspoon paprika
2 tablespoons chopped
  parsley
Salt to taste

Scrub clean, dry well and bake in 400° or no. 6 oven about 50 minutes. Take out and cut potatoes in half lengthwise and remove as much cooked potato as possible without breaking the skin and place in a bowl. Mash, add all other ingredients and beat well together. Put back into potato shells and place in a baking dish. Heat in 350° or no. 4 oven for about 15 minutes.

If garlic is not liked, ¼ cup of finely chopped green onion may be used.

serves 4

German Baked Stuffed Potatoes

6 large potatoes
¼ pint sour cream
1 egg beaten
4 oz chopped ham
1 chopped onion
½ pint stock

Boil potatoes in skins until soft, (30 minutes), cut in half lengthwise, scoop out centre and mash. Add ham, onion, egg and half the sour cream. Stuff the potatoes with this mixture and put them in a greased baking tin. Add the stock and rest of sour cream. Cover and bake in 350° or no. 4 oven for 30 minutes. Serve the gravy separately.

serves 6

Baked Potatoes Cooked with Beef

4 large potatoes
1 cup cooked minced beef
2 tablespoons butter
3 tablespoons milk
1 egg beaten
2 teaspoons chopped
  parsley
2 teaspoons chopped
  onion

Wash and dry potatoes. Bake at 400° or no. 6 oven for 1 hour. Take out of oven and cut small piece off top lengthwise and scoop out potato. Mash in bowl and add butter, milk, egg, beef onion and parsley. Beat all well together and fill the 4 cases. Heat in 350° or no. 4 oven for 20 minutes.

serves 4

Baked Potatoes with Broad Beans

6 large potatoes
1½ cups broad beans
3 tablespoons butter
¼ cup cream
Salt and peper to taste

Scrub clean and dry potatoes. Bake in 400° or no. 6 oven for 1 hour. Take out, cut in half lengthwise and scoop out all the potato, leaving the skin cases whole. Mash potato, add butter, cream, salt and pepper and fill cases. Make hole in centre and fill the 12 centres with broad beans. Reheat at 350° or no. 4 oven for 20 minutes.

serves 6

French Baked Potatoes

6 large potatoes
Butter
Salt and pepper

Scrub and dry potatoes, prick with fork and rub with oil. Bake at 400° or no. 6 for 1 hour.
   Serve whole in their skins, with salt and pepper and lots of butter.

serves 6

Baked Potatoes with Oysters

6 medium potatoes
¼ cup evaporated milk
6 large oysters
French dressing
4 tablespoons butter
½ teaspoon paprika
½ cup buttered
  breadcrumbs
Salt and pepper to taste

Scrub and dry potatoes, bake in 350° or no. 4 oven for 50 minutes. Remove from oven and cut a thin piece, about 2 inches lengthwise carefully. Remove the inside of potato and mash in bowl. Add butter, salt, pepper, paprika and evaporated milk and mash together. While the potatoes are cooking, marinate the oysters in a little French dressing (see receipe page 75) for about 30 minutes.
   Stuff the mashed potato back into the skins and put the drained oysters just down on the top of each potato, cover with breadcrumbs and place on baking dish. Cook in 350° or no. 4 oven for 25 minutes.

serves 6

Baked Potatoes with Vienna Sausages

4 large potatoes
8 Vienna sausages
3 tablespoons butter
4 tablespoons cream
Salt and peper to taste

Scrub and dry potatoes. Bake in 400° or no. 6 oven for 50 minutes. Take out, cut in half lengthwise, scoop out potato, being careful not to break the skin and mash in bowl. Add butter and cream, salt and pepper and fill the 8 shells. Place sausage along top of each shell. Put back in oven 350° or no. 4 for 20 minutes. If Vienna is not cooked enough, place under grill for few minutes.

serves 4

Baked Potatoes Cheese Souffle

6 large potatoes
4 tablespoons butter
¼ cup cream
½ cup grated Cheddar
   cheese
4 egg yolks beaten
4 egg whites
Salt and pepper to taste

Scrub and dry potatoes. Bake at 400° or no. 6 for 50 minutes. Take out of oven and cut small layer off top lengthwise. Scoop out as much potato as possible without breaking the skin. Mash with butter, cream, egg yolks, salt and pepper and cheese, keeping back 1 tablespoon. Beat egg whites until stiff and fold into potato mixture. Carefully fill the 6 cases and sprinkle with remaining tablespoon of grated cheese. Immediately place on baking dish and into 350° or no. 4 oven for 20 minutes.

serves 6

Baked Potato Puffs

4 large potatoes
2 tablespoons butter
¾ cup evaporated milk
2 egg yolks
2 egg whites
Salt and pepper to taste

Scrub and dry the potatoes and bake at 350° or no. 4 for 1 hour. Take out, slice small piece off the potato lengthwise and scoop all the potato out without breaking the skin. Mash, add butter, milk and egg yolks, salt and pepper. Beat egg whites until stiff and fold into potato mixture. Fill potato cases with mixture and cook in 350° or no. 4 oven for 20 minutes.

serves 4

Baked Potatoes Stuffed with Cheese

6 medium size potatoes
6 thick slices cheese
6 slices bacon

Wash and dry potatoes, bake in 400° or no. 6 oven for 45 minutes. Take out, split half way down centre and place piece of cheese and slice of bacon and place back in oven for another 15 minutes. Serve with salt and pepper and lots of butter.

serves 6

Pork Sausage in Baked Potatoes

6 long large potatoes
6 sausages
Melted butter
Paprika and salt

Wash and dry potatoes and bake in 400° or no. 6 oven for 45 minutes. Take out, peel, and with sharp knife cut hole the size of sausage down through centre and put the sausage down the centre. Place in baking dish, brush with melted butter and sprinkle with paprika and salt. Bake again at 350° or no. 4 for 30 minutes.

serves 6

Baked Potatoes with Cooked Lamb

6 medium potatoes
1 cup minced cooked
    lamb
3 tablespoons butter
1 small finely chopped
    onion
1 teaspoon chopped mint

Wash and dry potatoes and bake at 350° or no. 4 for 1 hour. Take out and cut 1½ inches thinly off top lengthwise. Scrape out potato and mash. Add butter, lamb, onion and mint and beat well together. Fill the 6 potato cases with mixture and reheat at 350° or no. 4 for 20 minutes.

serves 6

Granada Baked Potatoes

6 large potatoes
½ cup fresh breadcrumbs
1 cup flaked fresh fish
1 egg beaten
1 clove garlic crushed
6 tablespoons oil
1 tablespoon capers
½ cup cream
Pepper and salt to taste

Boil potatoes in skins for 20 minutes, peel and let cool. Cut in half and scoop out a good 1 inch wide and deep both sides. Boil fish for about 5 minutes, finely crumble and add to breadcrumbs, pepper and salt and egg and mash to paste.

Stuff centre of each half of potato and press them together again. Place in casserole or baking dish close together. Pour 1 tablespoon oil over each potato and sprinkle with garlic.

Bake in 400° or no. 6 oven for 20 minutes. They will be golden brown on each side. Take out and sprinkle with capers. Pour cream over, put back in oven for 5 minutes. Serve with sauce poured over them.

serves 6

Fried Potatoes

Pommes Frit or Game Chips

8 large potatoes
Cooking oil
Salt

Peel and cut potatoes in long ½-inch strips, soak them in cold water for 1 hour, dry thoroughly on clean towel. Heat oil until you see blue smoke. Drop in half the potatoes and cook until golden brown (3 to 5 minutes), lift out on to absorbent paper and put into warm oven until other half is cooked. Sprinkle with salt and serve. It is much easier if you have a wire basket to plunge into hot oil.

serves 8

Cottage Fried Potatoes

6 large potatoes
1 onion, minced
Fat for frying
Salt and pepper to taste

Boil the potatoes and peel, let them get cold. Cut the potatoes in slices (cucumber cutter is preferred). Have a lot of hot fat in frying pan, put potatoes in with onion, salt and pepper; saute until brown, shaking pan occasionally. Drain on paper and serve.

serves 6

Potatoes À La Lyon

24 small new potatoes
(otherwise, cut old ones
    into balls)
2 egg yolks, well beaten
2 teaspoons vinegar
1 teaspoon French
    mustard
3 tablespoon fat
Salt and pepper to taste

Boil potatoes until just cooked, drain and let cool. Heat fat to 380°and fry potatoes until brown, about 5 minutes; shaking pan occasionally. Lift out and drain an absorbent paper. To the hot fat then add vinegar, salt, pepper and mustard and mix well; shake pan for 3 minutes, add egg yolks, shake and serve over fried potatoes.

serves 4

Shoestrong Potatoes

These are delicious and dainty as an accompaniment with an entree.

The potatoes are cut thin as matchsticks and fried in hot, deep fat (395°) for about 3 minutes, drained and served.

Spanish Fried Potatoes

6 large potatoes
1 clove garlic
6 tablespoons oil
½ teaspoon minced onion
Salt to taste

Peel and slice potatoes ½-inch thick. Place in basin of cold water. Cut garlic and rub all over pan. Heat oil; drain and dry potatoes, add to oil with onion and cook slowly, turning occasionally so that potatoes cook evenly on all sides, taking about 25 to 30 minutes.

serves 4

American Hash Brown Potatoes

2 cups cooked potatoes
   chopped
1 tablespoon flour
3 tablespoons fat
Salt and pepper to taste

Sprinkle flour, salt and pepper over potatoes. Heat fat in frying pan, add potatoes and press down with spatula or broad knife. Cook until well brown on one side. Then turn over with egg lifter and brown well on other side. Serve at once.

serves 4

Lyonnaise Potatoes

2 cups boiled potatoes,
   diced
1 tablespoon parsley,
   chopped
1 teaspoon onion, minced
3 tablespoons butter
Salt and pepper to taste

Melt butter and fry onion until golden brown; add potatoes and toss lightly with a fork until they are brown on all sides trying not to break up the dices. Serve on hot plate sprinkled with parsley.

serves 4

American Southern Fried Potatoes

6 medium potatoes
1 egg beaten
Dry breadcrumbs
Fat for frying

Peel and cut potatoes ¼-inch thick slices, dip in egg and breadcrumbs and drop in hot melted fat, 380°. Cook about 7 minutes until brown, Drain on absorbent paper but serve hot.

serves 4

Twice Cooked Potatoes

6 boiled potatoes
Salt
Fat for frying

Cut potatoes ½-inch thick; heat deep hot fat to about 380°F, drop potato slices into fat and fry until golden brown and crisp. Drain on absorbent paper and serve hot.

serves 4

Potato Chips

8 medium potatoes
Salt
Fat for frying

Peel and cut potatoes into ½-inch strips, soak in cold water and dry well. Heat very deep fat to about 380°F; drop potato strips in—there should be enough room for them to move about—shake the pan while cooking. Cook until light brown, about 5 minutes after fat has come to boil again.

serves 6

Different ways to serve potato chips

They can be served with grated parmesan cheese.
They can be sprinkled with chopped chives or parsley.
They can be served with tomato ketchup.

French Fried Potatoes

6 potatoes
Deep fat for frying
Salt

Scrub potatoes well and cut in long ¼-inch strips unpeeled. Soak in cold water 1 hour, drain and dry well in towel. Heat deep fat to 395°F (if a 1-inch cube of bread browns in 20 seconds, the fat is hot enough) and drop dry chips in; heat until golden brown, about 5 minutes. You can put a fork through one to see if they are cooked.

Try them unpeeled, they are very good.

serves 6

Fried Diced Potatoes

8 large potatoes
⅓ cup peanut or
   vegetable oil
5 tablespoons butter
Salt

Peel potatoes, cut off sides and ends to make them into a square (you can save the cut off pieces for mashed potato). Cut into ¼-inch lengthwise, stack them and cut in ¼-inch squares. Soak in cold water, drain, then run boiling water over them. Dry well. Heat oil and 1 tablespoon butter in frying pan. Cook, stirring them, for 6 minutes. Drain on absorbent paper and clean frying pan. Melt remaining butter, add potatoes and cook for further 6 minutes, shaking the pan until nicely brown and crisp all over. Sprinkle with salt and serve immediately.

serves 6

Potatoes in Cream Sauce

The Broker Potato

2 cups cooked 1 inch
　diced potatoes
2 cups white sauce
Salt and pepper
Buttered breadcrumbs

Mix lightly the potatoes in white sauce with salt and pepper. Pour into buttered casserole and cover with buttered breadcrumbs. Cook in 425°F or no. 7 oven for 20 minutes.

serves 6

The Potato of Russia

4 medium potatoes
1 small onion,
　chopped finely
Boiling water
2 tablespoons butter
3 tablespoons sour cream
Salt and pepper

Peel potatoes and cut into large 1-inch pieces. Cook with onion, pepper and salt, with just enough water to cover. Simmer with lid on for about 30 minutes, or until tender; drain well, then add butter and cream and shake gently in saucepan until all is well mixed.

serves 4

Potatoes in Cheese Sauce

10 or 12 new potatoes
1 cup white sauce
1 tablespoon diced
　pimento
⅓ cup grated cheese

New potatoes are best for this, but any others will do, cut into 1½-inch pieces.

　Mix white sauce with added cheese. Cook potatoes in skins, peel after cooking; add cheese sauce and pimento and stir all gently so as not to break potatoes.

serves 4

Greek Potatoes and Garlic Sauce

6 medium potatoes
5 cloves garlic
1 teaspoon salt
¾ cup olive oil
¼ cup lemon juice

Boil potatoes in jackets. If you have no garlic crusher, chop garlic finely and pound to paste with salt until smooth. Peel potatoes, adding one at a time to garlic, mashing together into a smooth paste; then add olive oil very slowly, alternating with lemon juice, until you have a smooth mixture. When ready to serve, it might be diluted with a little fish or vegetable stock and heated.

　This sauce is excellent with fish, and also very good with zucchini, red beets or eggplant.

serves 0

Cream Potatoes

6 cups cooked potatoes,
    cubed
2 tablespoons butter
2 tablespoons flour
Dash of mace
Dash of cayenne
1 teaspoon salt
2 cups milk
½ teaspoon lemon juice

Melt butter, add flour, mace, cayenne and salt and blend together; add milk gradually, stirring all the time until thickened. Add lemon juice and potatoes, stirring gently until heated through.

serves 6

Spanish Potato Sauce

½ lb potatoes
2 tomatoes
1 red pepper
2 cloves garlic
2 tablespoons oil
1 bay leaf
1 clove
1 pint boiling water
Salt to taste

This potato sauce is served mainly with fish dishes.
    Chop all the vegetables very fine and cook slowly in oil until soft; then add water, bay leaf, clove and salt, stirring all the time until boiling. Turn down and simmer for about 10 minutes, then put in blender or through a sieve, reheat and serve. It can be kept and reheated later.

Creamed Steamed Potatoes

6 medium potatoes
Melted fat   .
1 teaspoon salt
1 cup water
1½ cups white sauce
Chopped parsley

Peel potatoes, brush all over with melted fat. Place in a baking dish and sprinkle with salt, add water and cover tightly and steam in 300° or no. 2 oven for 2½ hours. Then place the potatoes in a serving dish, cover with hot white sauce and sprinkle with parsley.

serves 6

Potatoes in Malaga Sauce

4 potatoes
2 green peppers
2 small onions
2 tablespoons pimento
1 cup milk
4 tablespoons butter
2 tablespoons flour
2 tablespoons grated
  Cheddar cheese
Salt and pepper to taste

Peel potatoes and cut in thin match-like strips, about ¼-inch thick. Cook in boiling water for 15 minutes, drain and keep warm.

Cut onion in rings and green peppers in ½-inch length thin slices. Fry onion in butter until brown; when half cooked, add green peppers. Then add flour, pimento, salt and pepper, blend together, add milk gradually, stirring constantly until thickened. Pour over potatoes and sprinkle with cheese.

serves 4

Creamed New Potatoes with Parsley

12 small new potatoes
½ cup milk
2 tablespoons butter
½ teaspoon salt
Dash of cayenne
1 tablespoon parsley,
  chopped

Boil potatoes in skins, cook in water until tender, about 20 minutes. Drain and peel. Put back in pan and pour milk on them. Cook until milk is absorbed; add butter, salt and cayenne and parsley; toss gently together.

serves 4

Creamed Potatoes in Salmon Sauce

6 medium potatoes
4 tablespoons butter
2 tablespoons flour
1 cup flaked salmon
1 cup milk
Salt and pepper to taste

Peel and cut potatoes in large cubes, about ¾-inch. Cook in water for about 15 to 20 minutes, until tender; drain and keep warm. Melt butter, add flour, salt and pepper, stir until blended; add milk gradually, stirring until thickened, add salmon and pour over potatoes.

serves 6

Caramel Potatoes

3 cups raw potatoes,
  grated
2 tablespoons butter
2 tablespoons flour
2 cups milk
Salt and pepper to taste

Melt butter, add flour, salt and pepper, blend well, add milk gradually, stirring all the time. Add grated potato and pour into well greased casserole; dot with little extra butter and bake in 325° or no. 3 oven for 3½ hours, or until caramel glaze forms on top of potatoes.

serves 4

Creamed New Potatoes with Bacon and Cheese

8 medium new potatoes
1 cup milk
2 tablespoons butter
2 tablespoons flour
4 slices bacon
½ cup grated cheese
Salt and pepper to taste

Cook potatoes in boiling water until tender, drain and peel and cut each potato into 4 pieces.

Fry bacon until crisp, remove from pan, drain on absorbent paper and crumble.

To bacon fat add butter, melt, then flour, salt and pepper and blend. Add milk gradually, stirring until thickened. Add bacon and nearly all the cheese (save 1 tablespoonful). Add potatoes and stir gently. Place in serving dish and sprinkle with rest of cheese.

serves 4

Creamed Potatoes with Spanish Sauce

4 medium potatoes
½ cup cooked ham,
    chopped
1 tablespoon green
pepper,
    chopped
½ tablespoon onion
    chopped
2 cups white sauce
Salt and paprika

Peel and cook potatoes until tender, about 25 to 30 minutes, drain and cut in ¾-inch cubes.

Boil the green pepper and onion in little water for 5 minutes. Drain and add to white sauce, add salt and paprika and heat; gently stir in potatoes and ham.

serves 4

Creamed Potatoes with Mustard Sauce

4 fairly large potatoes
2 tablespoons French or
    German mustard
2 tablespoons butter
½ pint stock
2 tablespoons
    breadcrumbs
1 tablespoon flour
Salt and pepper to taste

Peel and cook potatoes in boiling water until cooked but still firm. Drain and slice about ¼-inch thick. Place in greased oven dish. Melt 1 tablespoon butter, stir in flour, salt and pepper and blend. Add stock gradually, stirring all the time; add mustard, stir until dissolved. Pour sauce over potatoes and sprinkle with breadcrumbs. Dot with remaining 1 tablespoon butter, cook in oven or under grill until golden brown.

serves 6

Scalloped Potatoes

Scalloped Potatoes

6 medium potatoes
3 tablespoons butter
3 tablespoons flour
Milk
Salt and pepper to taste

Peel and cut potatoes into thin slices, grease a casserole dish and place layers of potatoes, sprinkling each layer with salt and pepper and dot with butter; fill until all potatoes are used, finish dotting with butter, pour milk over until it just reaches the top of the potatoes. Cook covered in 350°F or no. 4 oven for 1¼ hours, remove cover for last 15 minutes to let brown. Insert knife down centre of potatoes to make sure they are cooked.

serves 4

Scalloped Potatoes with Onion

8 medium potatoes
2 medium onions
Paprika and salt
4 tablespoons butter
4 tablespoons flour
Milk

Peel and cut potatoes in thin slices, cut onions in thin slices. Grease casserole, place layer of potatoes and thin layer of onion, sprinkling each layer lightly with salt, paprika and flour and dot with butter, keep filling with same layers, also dot top layer with butter. Pour milk over until just below top layer, cover with lid. Cook in 350° or no. 4 oven for 1½ hours.

serves 6

Scalloped Potatoes with Ham and Pimento

8 potatoes
4 tablespoons butter
4 tablespoons flour
Milk
2 tablespoons pimento, chopped
Large 1-inch thick slice of ham
Salt and pepper

Peel and slice thin the potatoes; place layer in buttered casserole, sprinkle with salt, pepper, flour and a little pimento and dot with butter; repeat layers until all is used, pour over milk to just below the top; then place the large slice of ham on top and cover. Cook in 350°F or no. 4 oven for 1½ hours. The ham can be cut into pieces and this will make a meal.

serves 4

Scalloped Potatoes Au Gratin

8 medium potatoes
1 cup grated cheese
3 tablespoons butter
3 tablespoons flour
1 pint cream
Salt and pepper to taste

Grease a casserole dish, bottom and sides.

Peel and slice potatoes ¼-inch thick, place layer in casserole, sprinkle with little cheese, flour, salt and pepper and dot all over with little butter. Keep repeating these layers, finishing with cheese. Pour cream over, cover casserole and cook in oven 350°F or no. 4 for 1¼ hours.

serves 6

Scalloped Potatoes with Layers of Ham or Chopped Bacon

6 potatoes
3 tablespoons finely
   chopped cooked ham or
   3 tablespoons finely
   chopped cooked bacon
3 tablespoons butter
3 tablespoons flour
Salt and paprika to taste
Milk

Peel and slice potatoes ⅛-inch thick, grease a casserole well. Place in layers of potatoes, sprinkle each layer with ham or bacon, flour, salt, paprika and dot with butter. Repeat until all is used. Pour milk until just before top, cover and cook in 375°F or no. 5 oven for 1 hour.

serves 4

Scalloped Potatoes with Mushroom

4 cups thinly sliced
   potatoes
1 can mushroom soup
¾ cup evaporated milk
½ cup water
¼ cup grated cheese
2 tablespoons finely
   chopped pimento
½ teaspoon salt

Grease casserole dish. Mix in large bowl mushroom soup, evaporated milk, water, cheese, pimento and salt. Then add potatoes. Pour all into casserole, cover and bake in 350°F for no. 4 oven for 1¼ hours. A few chopped fresh mushrooms can be added to this if in season.

serves 6

Scalloped Potatoes with Mixed Herbs

6 medium potatoes
2 shallots or spring onion, chopped (green tops too)
2 teaspoons mixed herbs
½ teaspoon salt
Milk
3 tablespoons butter
2 tablespoons flour

Peel and slice potatoes just under ¼-inch thick. Wash and dry well. Toss them in flour and salt. Mix together the herbs and shallots or spring onions.

Grease casserole, put in layers of potatoes, sprinkle with mixed herbs and onion and dot with some of the butter. Repeat these layers until all is used up, finishing with dots of butter. Pour milk to within ¼-inch from top. Cover casserole and bake in 350°F for no. 4 oven for 1¼ hours. The cover may be taken off for the last 20 minutes to allow potatoes to brown a little on top.

serves 4

Scalloped Potatoes with Cheese and Peppers

8 potatoes
¾ cup finely chopped green peppers
1 cup grated cheese
2 cups milk
3 tablespoons butter
3 tablespoons flour
Salt
Pinch of cayenne

Peel and slice potatoes ⅛-inch thick slices. Grease casserole dish and place in good layer of potatoes, spinkle with some of the green peppers, cheese, little flour, salt and cayenne; dot with some butter. Repeat these layers until all used; then pour milk over and cover. Cook in 350°F or no. 4 oven for 1¾ hours.

serves 6

Potato Pancakes

American Potato Pancakes

8 medium potatoes
Cold meat stock
2 cups flour
2 large eggs, beaten
Salt and pepper to taste

Peel and grate potatoes and cover with cold water. Soak for about 5 minutes, drain and squeeze the gratings in a towel. To the quantity of the potato pulp, add same amount of beef stock; add eggs, salt and pepper, and 1 cup flour, beating well until all thoroughly mixed. Then add the extra 1 cup flour gradually, beating all the time until mixture reaches pancake thickness. Grease frying pan with either butter or bacon fat and pour in large spoonful of mixture either 3 or 4 times, depending on size of pan. Cook on both sides until crisp.

serves 4

Fluffy Potato Pancakes

2 cups grated potatoes
1 teaspoon salt
¼ teaspoon baking
   powder
4 eggs, separated
1 tablespoon flour

Soak the potatoes in cold water for 10 minutes, drain, and dry on a towel. Add egg yolks, beaten, then add baking powder, salt and flour and beat all well. Beat egg whites until stiff and fold into potato mixture. Pour large spoonsful on to greased pan, fry on both sides until golden brown.

serves 4

French Potato Pancakes

1 cup mashed potatoes
1 cup sifted flour
4 eggs, separated
½ teaspoon salt
2½ cups milk

Combine potatoes with flour and salt, beat egg yolks and add with milk. Stiffly beat egg whites and fold into potato mixture. Drop large spoonsful on to greased pan and fry until golden brown.

serves 4

German Potato Pancakes

1 lb raw grated potatoes
2 oz cooked mashed
   potatoes
½ cup milk
1 egg, beaten
pepper and salt to taste

Mix together the raw and cooked potatoes, add egg, salt, pepper, and milk and beat all well together. Heat a little fat in pan and pour in spoonsful of mixture, fry on both sides until golden brown. These are nice served with grated or sliced applies.

serves 4

Austrian Potato Pancakes

2 cups mashed potatoes
½ cup sauerkraut
3 eggs, beaten
1 cup flour
1 tablespoon butter,
    melted
1 cup milk

Chop up sauerkraut and add to mashed potatoes. Add flour, eggs, butter and milk. Mix well together. It should mix to nice pouring mixture.

Melt a little butter or margarine in large frying pan and pour a large spoonful of potato mixture into fat. You can cook 3 or 4 spoonfuls at one time. Turn so that they are light brown on both sides.

serves 6

Dutch Potato Pancakes

3 cups grated potatoes
4 eggs, separated
1 sour apple grated
½ teaspoon onion, grated
1 cup flour
½ teaspoon salt

Beat egg yolks, add to potatoes, add apple, onion, flour and salt. Beat egg whites until stiff and fold into potato mixture. Pour a large spoonful into well-greased hot pan and fry until golden brown on both sides.

serves 6

Potato Pancakes

3 cups grated raw
    potatoes
2 eggs, well beaten
1½ cups flour
1 cup milk
¼ teaspoon baking
    powder
1 teaspoon salt

Sieve flour, salt and baking powder together, add to potatoes; then add beaten eggs and milk and mix thoroughly. Drop a spoonful into well greased hot pan, fry on both sides until brown.

serves 6

Polish Potato Pancakes

2 cups mashed potatoes
1 cup milk
3 eggs, separated
3 tablespoons butter,
    melted
⅛ teaspoon nutmeg
1 teaspoon salt

Beat egg yolks, add milk and add to mashed potatoes
Add butter, nutmeg and salt. Beat egg whites until stiff and fold into potato mixture. Drop a large spoonful in greased hot pan and cook on both sides until browned.

serves 4

Potato Dumplings

Potato Dumplings

If mashed potato is to be used for dumplings, it is better and easier to manage if cooked the day before. In making the dumplings, add flour gradually as it may not all be needed.

German Potato Dumplings

2 cups mashed potato
1 egg, beaten
Salt and pepper to taste
3 tablespoons flour
3 slices bread
2 tablespoons butter

Mix the mashed potatoes with salt, pepper and flour, add egg and beat to a smoothe paste. Dice the bread in ½-inch squares and fry in butter until crisp. Put the potato paste on floured board and shape it into a long baton-like roll, cut into 1½-inch pieces, press a piece of fried bread into each and shape them in the form of dumplings. Drop into boiling hot water and cook for about 15 minutes. Take one piece out and cut through; if it is not soggy in the middle, the dumplings are done. Serve with melted butter.

Always leave enough room in saucepan so the dumplings can float on top and just steam. Keep tight lid on saucepan while cooking.

serves 4

Austrian Potato Dumplings

4 large cooked potatoes
2 heaped tablespoons
   minced ham
2 egg yolks
½ teaspoons chopped
   parsley
1 tablespoon melted
   butter
8 oz rice
2 tablespoons flour
Fat for frying
Pepper and salt to taste

Cook the rice so that it is dry and separated, add the rice and ham to potatoes and mix well, add melted butter, parsley, salt and pepper and bind together with egg yolks. Form into small balls with floured hands and fry in deep fat for 10 minutes. Either serve in soup or, if desired with main dish, with melted butter over them.

serves 4

Czech Potato Dumplings

1½ lb potatoes
2 eggs beaten
2 tablespoons vinegar
2 tablespoons semolina
8 oz plain flour
Salt

Use potatoes that have been boiled and peeled the day before. Grate them, add salt, eggs, vinegar, semolina and flour and knead until the dough is firm. Use immediately, form the dough into 4 rolls and put them into a large saucepan of boiling salted water. After a few minutes they will rise to the top, then cover and simmer for 20 minutes. Remove carefully and cut into 2 inch pieces. These are delicious served with roast meat.

serves 6

Irish Potato Dumplings

4 cups cold mashed
  potatoes
½ cup grated uncooked
  potato
2 tablespoons fat
1 tablespoon finely
  chopped onion
1 dessertspoon salt
¾ cup flour
2 lightly beaten eggs
Salt and pepper to taste

Fry onion in fat until golden brown, add uncoocked grated potato and cook until mixture forms a paste, let it cool. Add cooked potatoes, salt and pepper, flour and eggs and stir together until smooth. Form into balls, about the size of a walnut and drop into boiling salted water, cook until dumplings rise to top and are cooked through centre, about 15 minutes altogether.

These can be served with melted butter or in hot soup.

serves 6

Dutch Potato Dumplings

9 medium potatoes
⅔ cup fine breadcrumbs
1 cup flour
3 eggs, well beaten
1 teaspoon salt
½ teaspoon nutmeg

Boil potatoes in skin until tender, about 30 minutes, peel and mash with salt, nutmeg, breadcrumbs, flour and eggs, mix to smooth paste. Roll into pieces the size of walnut and drop into boiling salted water; when balls come to surface, allow them to cook for about 5 minutes. Lift out on to plate and keep hot. Serve with the mushroom dressing.

Mushroom dressing
3 tablespoons butter
½ cup breadcrumbs
2 tablespoons finely
   chopped onion
2 tablespoons finely
   chopped mushrooms

Melt butter, add onion and mushrooms, cook for about 10 minutes then add breadcrumbs and serve over top of dumplings.

serves 8

Plum Potato Dumplings

1 lb cooked potatoes
1 egg, beaten
2 oz flour
2 oz cornflour
12 to 16 small plums
¼ teaspoon nutmeg

For these dumplings, it is better to cook the potatoes the day before and mash them, as fresh cooked potatoes are inclined to come apart.

Mix potatoes, the flour and cornflour, nutmeg and egg to smooth paste, put paste on floured board and shape into long baton-like roll, cut into pieces of equal size. Take the stones out of plums and place a small cube of sugar in centre; press each piece of paste around the plum, making sure it is all evenly well covered. Drop into boiling water, cook for about 12 minutes. Serve sprinkled with fried breadcrumbs.

serves 4

Potato Croquettes

French Croquettes

2 cups hot mashed
   potatoes
¼ teaspoon celery salt
1 teaspoon chopped
   parsley
1 egg, well beaten
Breadcrumbs
2 tablespoons butter
1 teaspoon finely chopped
   onion
1 egg yolk, beaten
Salt and pepper to taste

Combine potatoes with, salt, pepper, celery salt, butter, parsley, onion and egg yolk and whip all together. Shape into cylinders about 2 inches long, dip into breadcrumbs, then into beaten egg, then into breadcrumbs again. Fry in hot fat, 380°F, until golden brown.

serves 6

Potato with Spinach Croquettes

2 cups hot mashed
   potatoes
½ cup cooked minced
   spinach
1 egg, well beaten
2 egg yolks, beaten
2 tablespoons butter
Breadcrumbs
Salt and pepper to taste

Add to hot potatoes, spinach, salt and pepper, and egg yolks, butter. Beat all together until well combined, shape into croquettes, dip in beaten egg and roll in breadrumbs. Fry in hot deep fat (380°F) until golden brown.

serves 6

Croquettes De Pommes De Terre

1½ cups hot mashed
   potatoes
½ cup minced cold roast
   beef
1 egg yolk beaten
1 tablespoon chopped
   parsley
1 small onion,
   finely chopped
1 egg white
Salt and pepper to taste

Combine potatoes with beef, parsley, onion, egg yolk, salt and pepper, chill in refrigerator for at least 30 minutes. Then shape into croquettes, dip in egg white, and fry in deep hot fat, 380°F; until golden brown.

serves 4

Filled Potato Croquettes

2 cups hot mashed
  potatoes
3 tablespoons cream
½ teaspoon salt, dash of
  cayenne
1 teaspoon finely chopped
  onion
1 egg yolk
½ cup finely chopped
  meat
3 tablespoons brown
  gravy
1 egg, beaten
Fine dry breadcrumbs
Fat for frying

Combine potatoes, cream, salt, cayenne, onion and egg yolk and mix well together. Combine meat and gravy. Shape potato mixture into little nests and put a little of the meat mixture into each one, cover with extra potato mixture and roll into 1¼ inch sausage rounds; flatten ends, dip in egg and roll in breadcrumbs. Drop in hot deep fat, about 380°F, until golden brown.

serves 4

Potato Croquettes with Fish Filling

4 cups hot mashed
  potatoes
2 egg yolks
2 teaspoons finely
  chopped chives or
parsley
1 tablespoon evaporated
  milk
½ cup cooked flaked fish
1 tablespoon tartare sauce
1 egg, beaten
Fine dry breadcrumbs
Fat for frying

Mix potatoes, egg yolks, chives or parsley and evaporated milk, beat all well together. Mix fish and tartare sauce. Make a little nest of potato, filling each with a little of fish, covering with little more potato, roll lengthwise and flatten ends; dip in egg and breadcrumbs and fry in deep hot fat until golden brown.

serves 6

Croquettes Pommes De Fromage

2 cups mashed potatoes
2 tablespoons Gruyere
   cheese, grated
1 egg
2 tablespoons melted
   butter
1 teaspoon parsley,
   chopped
Salt and pepper to taste
Breadcrumbs

Mix well together potatoes, cheese, butter, parsley, salt and pepper, form into croquettes about 2 inches long, flattening the ends; dip into egg and breadcrumbs. Fry deep in hot fat about 380°F until golden brown.

serves 4

Potato-Chicken Croquettes

4 cups mashed potatoes
1 tablespoon melted
   butter
2 egg yolks
1 tablespoon flour
½ cup cooked minced
   chicken
1 egg, beaten
Salt and pepper to taste
Breadcrumbs

Mash well together potatoes, butter, egg yolks, flour, chicken, salt and pepper, roll out about 2 inches long and 1¼ inches thick; dip in egg and roll in breadcrumbs. Drop into hot deep fat and fry until golden brown.

serves 6

Potato Cakes and Patties

Potato Cakes as a Meal

2 cups mashed potatoes
(warm)
2 onions sliced
2 tablespoons grated
cheese
2 tablespoons butter
3 tomatoes, sliced
6 eggs
Fat for frying
Pepper and salt to taste

Add to mashed potatoes butter, salt, pepper, and cheese and mix well together. Shape into round, flat cakes and fry in hot fat; drain on absorbent paper. To a little fat, add the onion and brown, and tomatoes and cook for about 15 minutes. Pour this over the potato cakes and serve with fried egg on top.

This is good for a lunch or Sunday night supper.

serves 4

Potato Patties with Mushrooms

4 cups mashed potatoes
2 onions, chopped fine
1 cup breadcrumbs
4 oz or small can
mushrooms, sliced thin
2 tablespoons butter
2 eggs, well beaten
Oil for frying
Salt and pepper to taste

Fry onion in butter, add sliced mushrooms, salt and pepper and cook until no liquid remains. Make small potato rounds and push hole in centre of each, put a little of the onion and mushroom mixture in and fold over, making sure to cover all the mixture. Brush the patties with egg and cover with breadcrumbs and fry in hot oil until crisp. Serve with tomato sauce.

serves 6

Australian Potato Cakes

½ lb cooked potatoes
3 oz flour
½ teaspoon baking
powder
¼ teaspoon salt
Pepper
1 oz butter
1 dessertspoon milk
3 oz bacon

Cut each strip of bacon into 3 lengthwise, roll each strip and secure with toothpick and fry in frying pan until cooked; remove and keep hot in oven, leave fat in pan.

Sift flour with baking powder, salt and pepper and mix in butter with finger tips until crumbly. Mash and add potatoes and milk; mix to a stiff dough, knead it a little and roll out ¼-inch thick; using a cutter if possible, cut into rounds or half-moon shapes.

Melt butter with bacon fat and fry the cakes gently on each side until golden brown and garnish with bacon rolls.

serves 4

Salmon Potato Cakes

6 cups cooked potatoes,
    chopped
2 cups flaked salmon
1 green pepper, chopped
1 egg, beaten
Fat for frying
Chopped parsley

Combine all ingredients together and form into little cakes about 2½ inches in diameter and ½-inch thick, and fry in fat until browned on both sides, sprinkle with parsley and serve with tartare sauce or lemon.
    serves 6

Potato and Onion Cakes

3 cups mashed potatoes
2 tablespoons finely
    chopped onion
1 egg beaten
Salt and pepper to taste
Fat for frying

Mix potatoes, onion, salt, pepper and egg to smooth mixture and shape into cakes 3 inches in diameter, ½-inch thick and fry on both sides until well browned.
    serves 4

Potato Patties with Cheese

6 medium potatoes
2 tablespoons flour
2 tablespoons butter
1 heaped tablespoon
    grated Swiss cheese
Salt and pepper to taste

Cook potatoes for 30 minutes, mash, add flour, butter salt, pepper and cheese and mix well together; shape into little patties. Bake on a greased baking dish in 400°F or no. 6 oven until golden brown on both sides, about 25 to 30 minutes.
    serves 4

American Potato Cakes

4 cups mashed potatoes
1 dessertspoon chopped
    parsley
1 tablespoon butter
1 egg beaten
Salt and pepper to taste
Crushed cornflakes
Fat for frying

Mix potatoes, parsley, butter, salt, pepper and egg well together. Form into little cakes and turn each side into crushed cornflakes; fry each side in hot fat until golden brown.
    serves 4

Australian Potato Cakes

1½ lb boiled potatoes
2 tablespoons parsley, chopped
1 tablespoon mint, chopped
1 tablespoon chives, chopped
½ teaspoon sage
¼ teaspoon marjoram
2 tablespoons butter
½ cup grated cheese
2 eggs, separated
Salt and pepper to taste

Mash potatoes while still warm. Saute all herbs in butter for few minutes; add to potatoes with cheese, salt and pepper and stir in slightly beaten egg yolks. Beat egg whites until stiff and fold into potato mixture, put into a well-greased 7-inch spring pan or cake pan and bake in 375°F or no. 5 oven for 35 minutes; turn out on platter, serve with parsley around edge.

saerves 6

Australian Potato Patties

1 lb potatoes
1 tablespoon butter
2 tablespoons flour
1 teaspoon salt
Fat for frying
½ teaspoon caraway

Peel and cut potatoes coarsely, cook in boiling salted water for 12 minutes, drain, put through ricer or sieve into a bowl, add salt, butter and flour and mix to a dough; if still a little sticky, add a little more flour. Roll into a ball and put on a floured board, roll out ¼-inch thick and cut into 3 inch squares, fry in hot fat, turning to make both sides golden brown and crisp. Serve with hot sauerkraut, in cup of brown sauce with ½ teaspoon caraway seeds added.

serves 4

Roast Potatoes

There are not too many recipes or ways for roasting potatoes.

Medium-size potatoes can be peeled and left whole; larger ones can be peeled and cut in half. Put in hot fat around roasting meat, turning at least once for browning.

Also, the potatoes can be peeled and boiled for 3 or 4 minutes, drained, then put around the joint or roast of meat. This method makes them crisp outside and fluffy inside.

It is usual to roast potatoes for 1 or 1½ hours, depending upon how high you have your oven for whatever meat you are roasting.

I have had roast potatoes done in another way; with large potatoes, thinly peeled, and brushed all over with melted fat, then placed on greased oven sheet or baking dish and cooked for 1½ hours in 350°F or no. 4 oven.

Potato Soups

Potato Soup

3 medium potatoes,
   chopped
3 medium onions,
   chopped
½ cup celery, chopped
3 cups water
1 cup milk
2 tablespoons butter
Chopped parsley
Salt and paprika

Boil potatoes, onion and celery in water for ½-hour, then put in blender or through sieve, put back in pan, add butter, milk, salt and paprika, heat and serve with parsley sprinkled on top.

serves 6

Potato Soup with Tomatoes

2 cups diced potatoes
2 cups diced onion
2 cups tomatoes, peeled
   and diced
3 tablespoons butter
¼ teaspoon thyme
2 teaspoons sugar
4 cups water
1 cup cream
Salt and pepper to taste

Fry onions in butter until soft, add potatoes, tomatoes, sugar, thyme, salt and pepper and water; bring to boil and simmer for 20 minutes, add cream, heat but do not boil again.

serves 8

Cream of Potato Soup

3 large potatoes
1 medium onion
1 stick celery
1 teaspoon mustard
2 cups thin white sauce
Salt and pepper

Peel and dice potatoes, chop onion, chop celery and add to 3 cups of water, bring to a boil, and cook for 30 minutes. Mash to a puree, or put in blender. Add the mustard, salt and pepper to white sauce, add all to puree and serve hot.

serves 6

Grated Potato Soup

6 potatoes, grated
6 cups chicken broth
1 onion, chopped
1 clove garlic, crushed
2 leeks, finely chopped
Pepper and salt to taste

Add all ingredients to stock, being to boil, and cook for 30 minutes with lid on.

serves 8

Potato and Tuna Chowder

2 cups diced potatoes
1 tin (7 oz) tuna in oil
1 large onion, chopped
¼ teaspoon Tobasco sauce
1 cup water
1 tin (16 oz) creamed sweet corn
3 cups milk
2 tablespoons chopped parsley
1 teaspoon salt
1 tablespoon butter

Fry onion in butter until tender, but not brown. Add water and potatoes and cook with lid on for 15 minutes. Add sweet corn, tuna, tabasco sauce, salt and parsley. Stir well together, add milk and bring to boil.

serves 6

Potato and Tuna Potage

2 tablespoons chopped celery
2 tablespoons chopped green peppers
1 large onion, chopped
1 tablespoon butter
1 cup mashed potatoes
¼ teaspoon basil
1 tin tomato soup
1 cup water
1 cup milk
1 tin tuna (7 oz) drained and flaked
Salt and pepper to taste

Cook onion, green peppers in butter, add all the rest of ingredients, stir thoroughly together and heat.

serves 6

American Potato Soup

2 tablespoons butter
2 teaspoons chopped
   onion
2 teaspoons chopped
   parsley
2 teaspoons chopped
   celery
3 medium potatoes diced
1 quart boiling water
1 tablespoon flour
Salt and pepper to taste

Melt 1 tablespoon butter, add onion, parsley, celery, salt and pepper, simmer gently for 10 minutes, stirring occasionally; add potatoes and water and cook with lid on for 30 minutes. In another saucepan melt 1 tablespoon butter, add flour, brown slightly, add 1 cup of potato liquid until it thickens, then add to soup. Serve with croutons.

serves 4

Portuguese Potato Soup

2 cloves garlic, crushed
2 onions, chopped
2 tablespoons oil
4 cups celery chopped
2 tablespoons instant
   potato
4 poached eggs
1 small tin tomato paste
2 cups chicken stock
¼ teaspoon thyme
1 cup white wine
1 mild Portuguese
   sausage, cooked and
   cut in ½-inch slices
Salt and pepper to taste

Fry in oil the garlic, onion, then add celery, chicken stock, instant potato, tomato paste and wine, salt, pepper, thyme and sausage. Simmer gently for 30 minutes and pour into bowl over poached eggs. This is a meal in itself.

serves 4

Hungarian Potato Soup

3 cups diced potatoes
1 cup diced celery
½ cup chopped onion
½ cup diced pimento
2 cups water
2 tablespoons flour
4 tablespoons butter
4 cups, hot milk
Salt and pepper to taste

Cook in water potatoes, celery, onion, pimento, salt and pepper; bring to boil and simmer for 20 minutes.

Melt butter, add flour, then add hot milk gradually, stirring continuously, then added to potato mixture and cook for another 5 minutes.

serves 8

Potato Fish Chowder

1 lb good fish, cut in
  pieces
1 lb fish bones
½ lb salt pork
2 medium onions
2 large potatoes, peeled
  and diced
2 tablespoons whipped
  cream
1 quart milk
1 tablespoon butter
1 tablespoon flour
Salt and pepper to taste

Boil fish bones in 2 cups water for 30 minutes. Fry chopped salt pork and onion, strain water from fish bones over them and add diced potatoes, cook for 15 minutes.

In another, saucepan heat milk, add fish and simmer for 20 minutes, add to potato mixture.

Heat butter, add flour, simmer a few minutes, add 1 cup of hot soup, mix to smooth paste and add to soup, heat and add cream.

serves 6–8

Winter Soup

2 cups diced potatoes
1 large onion chopped
2 cloves garlic crushed
1 leek chopped fine
2 tablespoons chopped
  parsley
1 cup milk
4 pork sausages
6 slices bacon
2 cups chicken stock
1 tablespoon butter
1 tin evaporated milk
1 tablespoon flour
Pepper and salt to taste

Fry bacon until crisp and take out of pan. Fry sausages until cooked and take out of pan. Add 1 tablespoon butter and onion, garlic and leek and fry until soft, but not brown, transfer to large saucepan, add potatoes, parsley and 2 cups stock. Bring to boil and cook for 15 minutes, add salt and pepper and evaporated milk and bring to boil again. Cut each sausage into 5 or 6 pieces and coarsely crumble bacon, add to pot. Mix flour and milk until no lumps remain, add to pot stirring continuously until it comes to boil and is a little thick. A large bowl of this can be a meal.

serves 6

Dutch Potato Soup

6 medium potatoes diced
3 slices bacon, chopped
2 onions chopped fine
2 tablespoons chopped
  parsley
2 cups boiling stock
2 cups milk
Salt and pepper to taste

Fry bacon and onion for few minutes, add potatoes and water, simmer for 20 minutes; add salt and pepper and milk and cook until hot. Serve with parsley sprinkled on top.

serves 6

Curried Potato and Shrimp Potage

2 cups diced potatoes
2 cups stock
½ cup chopped onion
2 tablespoons flour
½ teaspoon curry powder
½ cup cream
2 tablespoons chopped
   parsley
2 tablespoons sherry
1 tablespoon butter
Salt and pepper to taste
2 oz shrimps (when cooked)

Melt butter, fry onion, add potatoes, parsley, stock, salt and pepper and cook for 20 minutes; add shrimps and sherry. Mix flour and curry with little water and mix into soup stirring continuous, gently, add cream, heat and serve.

serves 4

Potato and Salmon Chowder

1 cup mashed potatoes
1 cup cooked French
   beans
2 cups diced celery
½ cup flaked salmon
1 tablespoon butter
2 cups water
1 cup milk
Chopped parsley
Salt and pepper to taste

Cook celery in melted butter until tender, then add all other ingredients except parsley; mix well together and heat thoroughly. Garnish with parsley.

serves 4

Potato Chowder

2 cups diced potatoes
½ cup diced salt pork
1 cup diced turnip
1 cup diced carrot
2 cups boiling water
1 medium onion chopped
1 stalk celery chopped
1 green pepper diced
2 cups thin white sauce

Fry salt pork and all vegetables for 5 or 6 minutes, add boiling water and simmer for 30 minutes, add salt and pepper. Add cream sauce stirring continuously until hot.

serves 6

Potato Potage Pistou

2 medium potatoes,
   peeled and sliced
½ lb French beans, sliced
4 tomatoes, peeled
½ lb vermicelli
½ teaspoon salt
2 cloves garlic crushed
1 teaspoon basil
2 tablespoons oil
3 oz grated Gruyere
   cheese
2 pints boiling water

Add to boiling water beans, 2 tomatoes sliced and potatoes. Cook for 10 minutes, add vermicelli and simmer for 20 minutes. With the 2 remaining tomatoes, grill them and drain, add garlic and basal and salt; add oil drop by drop to the tomato mixtured, then pour on a couple spoonfuls of the hot soup, stirring as you do so; add tomato mixture to soup and heat. Add the cheese just before serving.

serves 6

Vichyssoise Soup

4 medium potatoes,
   chopped
3 leeks, chopped
1 onion, chopped
Chopped chives
2 tablespoons butter
4 cups chicken stock
1 cup cream
Salt and pepper to taste

This can be served hot or very cold. I prefer it ice cold.
   Fry onions and leeks in butter until cooked but not brown, add potatoes and stock and cook for 45 minutes. Put all in blender or through sieve, then add cream, salt and pepper and heat or put in refrigerator. Serve with chopped chives on top.

serves 6

German Potato Soup

1 lb potatoes, peeled and
   sliced
1 tablespoon butter
1 tablespoon flour
4 oz cooked sliced
   Mettwurst sausage
3 pints stock
1 cup milk
Salt and peper to taste
Dried mixed herbs

Cook potatoes in stock for 30 minutes, then put them in blender or through sieve and return to saucepan. In another pan melt butter, add flour, then add milk stirring continuously until thickened; add to soup, again stirring, add sausage, salt and pepper and heat. Serve with herbs sprinkled on top.

serves 6

Czech Potato Soup

6 medium potatoes,
   chopped
2 pints water
1 pint milk
1 teaspoon butter
1 egg yolk
Salt to taste
1 dessertspoon parsley

Garnish
1 oz flour
1 egg

First prepare the garnish, work the egg and flour
and little cold water to a stiff dough, grate on a clean
towel and leave to dry.

Boil potatoes in water and put in blender or pass
through sieve. Put back in saucepan, add milk, salt
and garnish, boil for 5 minutes. Whisk in fresh egg
yolk, butter and parsley⅓do not boil again.

serves 6

Potato Clam Chowder

2 cups potatoes, diced
4 slices bacon
1 onion chopped
2 cups water (if tinned
   clams)
3 tablespoons butter
3 tablespoons flour
2 cups milk
Salt and pepper to taste

Either use about 30 fresh clams, well scrubbed and
boiled in 3 cups water, saving the water and
chopping the clams up finely—or use a 12 or 16 oz
tin of clams, using the liquid as well.

Fry bacon and onion for few minutes, add water
and potatoes and cook for 15 minutes; add clams,
salt and pepper and heat. In another saucepan melt
butter, add flour, stir to paste, add milk gradually,
then add to clam mixture. This can be a meal in
itself, served with Saltina or Water Biscuits.

Manhattan Clam Chowder

This is the same as the previous recipe except
instead of using milk, you use 2 cups of tomato juice
and 1 or 2 chopped up tomatoes, maybe cooked
with potatoes if desired.

Potato Salads

Hot De Luxe Potato Salad

2 cups diced cooked
  potatoes
½ cup finely diced celery
2 hard-boiled eggs,
  chopped
1 cup shredded Cheddar
  cheese
2 tablespoon chopped
  onion
¼ cup breadcrumbs
½ cup mayonnaise
¼ teaspoon dry mustard
1 tablespoon vinegar
2 tablespoon water
Pepper and salt

It is always best for any potato salad to cook the potatoes in their jackets and peel after cooking.

Mix together mayonnaise, mustard, vinegar and water; add to potatoes, onions, celery and eggs; toss lightly and season to taste with pepper and salt. Place layers of potato mixture in casserole dish, sprinkled with cheese, finishing with a layer of cheese and breadcrumbs.

Bake in 350°F or no. 4 oven for 30 minutes.

serves 6

Moulded Potato Salad

1 tablespoon unflavoured
  gelatin
¼ cup cold water
2 teaspoons sugar
½ teaspoon salt
2 teaspoons lemon juice
2 teaspoons finely
  chopped onion
1 teaspoon chopped
  parsley
¼ cup chopped celery
2 cups diced cooked
  potato
½ cup mayonnaise
½ cup evaporated milk

Soften gelatin in cold water for 5 minutes, then dissolve over boiling water; add sugar, salt and lemon juice, then add celery, parsley, chopped onion and potatoes; place in refrigerator until it just begings to set; take out fold in mayonnaise and evaporated milk and mix thoroughly. Pour into a wet ring mold and refrigerate for a few hours; turn out on plate larger than mold. You can fill the centre with salmon or tuna and garnish around outside with lettuce or parsley.

serves 6

Potato Salad with Ham and Asparagus Rolls

12 stalks asparagus
12 slices ham
French dressing
   (see recipe page 00)
2 cups potato salad
Lettuce
Radish roses

Marinate the asparagus in French dressing, drain and roll each stalk in a thin slice of ham. Arrange rolls on a large round plate, with tips facing out to rim of plate. Place potato salad on lettuce leaves in centre, with some radish roses around the salad.

serves four

Simple Potato Salad

2 lb potatoes
2 eggs, hard-boiled and
   sliced
2 gherkins, chopped
1 large onion, chopped
1 green pepper, chopped
Marinade
4 tablespoons oil
1 tablespoon French
   mustard
1 teaspoon vinegar
1 teaspoon sugar
½ teaspoon salt

Cook potatoes in skins, peel and cut in ¼-inch slices, add to potatoes, gherkins, onion and green pepper. Mix marinade together and toss lightly into potato mixture; place in wide bowl and the sliced egg on top.

serves 6

Mashed Potato Salad

8 potatoes, cooked and
   mashed
3 eggs, hard-boiled and
   chopped
¼ cup green pepper,
   finely chopped
¼ cup onion, finely
   chopped
1 teaspoon parsley, finely
   chopped
Salt and pepper to taste
Mayonnaise, about 1 cup

Add to mashed potatoes all ingredients except mayonnaise and mix well together; add mayonnaise gradually until mixture is a nice moist consistency. Serve individual servings on crisp lettuce leaf with little radish rose at side.

serves 6

Potato Aspic Salad

2 cups mashed potato
   salad
2 packets gelatine
4 cups tomato juice
Parsley

Dissolve gelatine in a little of the tomato juice, bring rest of romato juice to boil, add gelatine, stirring well until all dissolved. Let it cool a little and pour half of it into an oiled loaf pan or mould, set in refrigerator. When almost set, put in layer of potato salad and pour remaining tomato juice over. Chill until set firm. Unmould on serving dish and serve with parsley around and one piece on top. Cut in 1 inch slices right through. *serves 8*

German Potato Salad (1)

1 lb potatoes
2 egg yolks, beaten
4 teaspoons oil
1 tablespoon tarragon
   vinegar
¼ cup red wine
1 teaspoon mustard
1 tablespoon green olives,
   finely chopped
4 anchovies, chopped
4 spring onions or
   shallots, chopped
1 tablespoon capers
4 tablespoons stock
Salt to taste

Stir in saucepan oil, vinegar, red wine, stock and mustard; add capers and spring onions, then stir in egg yolk until the dressing thickens. Cook potatoes in skins, when slightly cool, peel and cut into ¼-inch slices, add olives, anchovies, sprinkle with salt. Pour dressing over all, toss gently, place in serving bowl and chill.

serves 4

German Potato Salad (2)

1 lb potatoes
1 tart apple, grated
2 slices bacon, cooked
   crisp and crumbled
1 tablespoon mayonnaise
   dressing of (1) salad
Salt to taste

Cook potatoes in skins and peel while still warm; slice into ¼-inch slices, add apple and bacon, sprinkle with salt. Add mayonnaise to dressing and toss gently with potato mixture; place in serving bowl and chill.

serves 4

Dutch Potato Salad

3 cups cooked potatoes,
     sliced
1 onion, diced
4 slices bacon, fried crisp
     and crumbled
1 tablespoon parsley
1 tablespoon vinegar
1 tablespoon sugar
4 tablespoons mayonnaise
Salt and pepper to taste

In a bowl mix potatoes, onion, bacon, parsley,
vinegar, sugar, salt and pepper, toss lightly, add
mayonnaise, and mix through lightly and chill.

serves 6

Potato and Salami Salad

4 cups cooked potatoes,
     diced
1½ cups salami, cut into
     ¼ inch cubes
1 cup celery, chopped
     finely
¼ cup pimento, finely
     chopped
2 eggs, hard-boiled and
     chopped
6 gherkins, chopped fine
4 tablespoons mayonnaise
Salt and pepper to taste

Mix all ingredients together, lastly adding
mayonnaise, gently tossing mayonnaise through; if
you prefer salad a little moister, add more
mayonnaise. Chill several hours.

serves 6

Potato Salad Loaf

3 cups My Favourite
     Potato Salad
3 cups potato and salami
     salad
4 eggs hard-boiled
Butter
breadcrumbs
8 radish roses

Well butter a long loaf pan and cover bottom and
sides with breadcrumbs. Put in 1 cup of *My Favourite
Potato Salad* (page 76) and press down with back of
spoon, put in 1 cup potato and salami salad and
press down evenly with back of spoon; repeat these
layers twice more. Chill for 2 or 3 hours or overnight
if you like. Turn out on long oval dish, cut
hard-boiled eggs in half lengthwise, place egss and
radish roses around dish. Cut through in 1 inch
slices.

serves 8

Marinated Potato Salad

4 cups cooked potatoes,
    diced
1 onion, chopped fine
3 eggs, diced
1 tablespoon parsley,
    chopped
French dressing
Salt and pepper to taste
Mayonnaise
Tomato wedges

To potatoes, add onion, eggs, parsley, salt and
pepper and toss in enough French dressing to
moisten through and leave to marinate for 2 hours.
Serve on crisp lettuce leaves with wedges of tomato
and a little mayonnaise on top of each serving.

serves 6

Russian Potato Salad

2 cups new potatoes,
    cooked and cubed
1 onion chopped finely
1½ cups celery, chopped
    finely
6 radishes, chopped finely
1 tablespoon sesame
    seeds
1 cup Russian dressing
Salt and pepper to taste

Toast sesame seeds in oven for 5 minutes, or fry in
dry frying pan for few minutes, cool. Mix the
potatoes, onion, celery, radishes, sesame seeds, salt
and pepper and toss in Russian dressing. Chill for
1 hour.

serves 6–8

Russian dressing
No. 1   1 cup mayonnaise, ½ cup chilli sauce
No. 2   1 cup mayonnaise, ¼ cup chilli sauce,
¼ cup Indian Relish (substitute for Indian Relish is
¼ cup of mixed finely chopped celery, green
peppers and pimento)
No. 3   ¾ cup mayonnaise, 1½ tablespoons
horseradish, 3 tablespoons caviar

Regency Potato Salad

1½ lb new potatoes
3 tablespoons spring
    onion, chopped
½ cup peas, cooked
¼ cup tongue or ham,
    chopped
4 tablespoons mayonnaise
Salt and pepper to taste

Boil potatoes in skins, peel and cut in cubes; while
potatoes are still warm, add spring onions, peas,
tongue or ham, salt and pepper and mix with
mayonnaise. Place in serving dish and chill for
couple of hours.

serves 6

Creamy Mashed Potato Salad

6 large potatoes
3 eggs, hard-boiled and
    chopped
½ green pepper, chopped
    finely
1 tablespoon onion,
    chopped finely

Dressing
2 tablespoons cream
1 egg, well beaten
2½ tablespoons vinegar
1 teaspoon French mustard
1 teaspoon sugar
1 teaspoon salt

Cook potatoes in skins, peel and mash, mix in
hard-boiled eggs, green pepper and onion.
Dressing   In double boiler, put sugar, salt, mustard,
vinegar and beaten egg stir until thick, add cream
and mix into mashed potato mixture, blending
thoroughly, and chill. This is nice served on
individual lettuce leaves, lay little strip of pimento or
tomato over top to give little colour.

serves 6

Garden Potato Salad

3 cups potato, cooked and
    diced
¾ cup celery, chopped
½ cup cucumber,
    chopped
¼ cup onion, chopped
1 tablespoon parsley,
    chopped
2 radishes, sliced thinly
1 cup mayonnaise
Salt and pepper to taste

Mix all ingredients with potatoes and stir
mayonnaise in gently, chill for at least 2 hours.
Garnish with parsley.

serves 6

Pommes De Terre En Salade

4 cups potatoes, cooked
    and sliced
French dressing
Sliced hard-boiled eggs
Sliced gherkins
Lettuce leaves

Marinate sliced potatoes in enough French dressing
to just cover for 2 hours in refrigerator; drain and
serve on plate of lettuce leaves surrounded with
sliced egg and sliced gherkins.

serves 6

American Potato Salad

3 cups potatoes, cooked
  and diced
½ cup celery, finely
  chopped
1 tablespoon green
  pepper, chopped finely
1 tablespoon onion,
  chopped finely
1 egg, hard-boiled,
  chopped finely
5 tablespoons oil
1 tablespoon vinegar
½ teaspoon dry mustard
Salt and pepper to taste

Mix with potatoes, celery, green pepper, onion and egg, toss gently. Mix mustard with little vinegar, add rest of vinegar, salt and pepper and oil, pour over potato mixture and toss again gently together. Chill.

serves 6

Buffet Potato Salad

4 cups potatoes, cooked
  and cubed
1 cup celery, chopped
½ cup onion, chopped
1 cup tuna fish or salmon,
  flaked
1 tablespoon parsley,
  chopped
Salt and pepper to taste
1 cup mayonnaise

Mix all ingredients together and toss gently in mayonnaise, add little extra mayonnaise if desired.

Serve with devilled eggs and large tomato wedges.

This is easy to prepare beforehand, if having people in to play cards.

serves 6

Savoury Potato Salad

4 cups sliced hot cooked
potatoes
8 slices crisp cooked
bacon, crumbled
12 stuffed olives, sliced
1 teaspoon chopped
chives
½ cup French dressing
Salt and pepper
Lettuce
Onion rings

Combine the potatoes, bacon, olives, chives and
French dressing, toss lightly and season to taste with
salt and pepper. Cover and chill in refrigerator for
several hours. Serve on crisp lettuce and garnish
with onion rings.

serves 6

French dressing
¾ cup salad oil
¼ cup vinegar
1 teaspoon salt
1 teaspoon sugar
½ teaspoon paprika
¼ teaspoon dry mustard
¼ teaspoon pepper

Combine all these ingredients in jar with tight-fitting
lid and shake until thoroughly blended, then place
in refrigerator. Shake well each time before using.

My Favourite Potato Salad

3 cups cooked potato,
diced
1 onion, diced finely
1 tablespoon mint,
chopped finely
2 tablespoons parsley,
chopped finely
2 tablespoons mayonnaise
3 tablespoons oil
1 dessertspoon vinegar
1 dessertspoon sugar
Salt and pepper to taste

If you do not have a parsley cutter, chop mint,
parsley and sugar together on chopping board. Add
all ingredients to potatoes and mix well together
chill for several hours.

serves 6

Miscellaneous
Potato Recipes

Potato Anna

6 cups very thinly sliced
    potatoes
½ teaspoon salt
Pepper
½ cup butter, softened
Cold water

After slicing potatoes soak them in cold water, drain them and dry with a towel, sprinkle with ½ teaspoon salt and a little pepper. Use a well buttered casserole or buttered mould and arrange a layer of potatoes at the bottom and up the sides, spread about 1 tablespoon butter over layer; continue layers, buttering each, until all potatoes are used, spread butter over top layer. Bake in 425°F or no. 7 oven for 40 or 50 minutes or until sharp knife goes easily down through centre. Put a serving plate over casserole or mold and invert. Potatoes came out in an attractive moulded form, golden brown all over.

serves 6

Pommes Au Lard

6 medium potatoes
¼ lb lean bacon
2 oz butter
Pinch of thyme
2 tablespoons flour
½ pint stock or water
1 teaspoon shredded
    parsley
Salt and pepper

Wash, peel and quarter the potatoes. Dice the bacon and fry lightly in butter, stir in the flour and add stock or water, salt and pepper, and stir all together; add potatoes and simmer, covered for 1 hour.

serves 4

Pommes De Lyonnaise

6 medium potatoes
4 oz bacon
2 oz butter
½ teaspoon origano herb
2 tablespoons flour
½ pint of water
Pinch of cayenne pepper
Salt

Peel, wash and quarter potatoes. Melt butter in saucepan; dice bacon and fry in 2 oz butter until golden brown, stir in salt, cayenne and origano, add water, stir and add potatoes. Cover and simmer for 1 hour.

serves 4

Potatoes Au Gratin

6 cups potatoes, riced and
  hot
¼ cup grated cheese
½ cup buttered
  breadcrumbs
2 eggs well beaten
3 tablespoons butter
Salt to taste
½ teaspoon paprika

To hot riced potatoes add butter, salt and paprika
and eggs, beat well together and place in greased
casserole dish, cover with cheese and buttered
breadcrumbs. Bake in 350°F or no. 4 oven about
20 minutes.

serves 6

Potato Pudding

4 cups mashed potatoes,
  hot
2 tablespoons butter
1 small onion chopped
  finely
1 lb pork sausage meat
4 oz ham, minced
½ teaspoon sage
Salt and pepper to taste
Fine breadcrumbs

Mash into potatoes butter, salt and pepper. Grease a
pudding basin and coat all over with breadcrumbs,
place in ½ cup of potatoes, then a little of the
sausage meat, onion, ham and sage. Repeat these
layers finishing with potatoes, cover tightly with
aluminium foil and steam for about 1¼ hours. Turn
out and place 4 pieces of parsley at base. Serve with
thick tomato sauce in separate bowl.

serves 6

Toasted Potato Balls

3 cups cooked potato balls
2 eggs beaten
½ cup milk
1 cup breadcrumbs
Salt and pepper to taste
Fat for frying

Either use small new potatoes or cut Irish potatoes
with potato cutter, cook them in boiling salted water
until tender. Mix eggs, milk, salt and pepper, roll
balls in egg mixture, then in breadcrumbs. Fry in
good amount of fat in frying pan, shaking
occasionally, until golden brown.

serves 6

Salmon Potato Casserole

2 cups mashed potato
¼ cup grated cheese
1 tablespoon butter
2 cups flaked salmon
¼ cup milk
Salt and pepper to taste

Mash butter and milk into potatoes; add salt, pepper and salmon and mix well. Put into greased casserole dish and sprinkle grated cheese on top. Bake in 350°F or no. 4 oven for 30 minutes.

serves 6

Pork Sausages with Mashed Potatoes

3 cups hot mashed
    potatoes
2 tablespoons butter
½ cup milk
1 egg, well beaten
12 medium size pork
    sausages
Salt and pepper to taste

Add butter, milk, salt and pepper to hot mashed potatoes. Prick sausages about 8 times with sharp fork and put in bottom of casserole dish, cover all over with mashed potatoes and pour the beaten egg over the top. Cook in 350°F or no. 4 oven for 35 minutes. Can be served with tomato sauce.

serves 6

Spanish Potato Omelet

1 lb potatoes
1 large onion
6 eggs
½ cup oil for frying
Salt and pepper

Chop up onion and fry in oil until golden brown. Peel and dice potatoes and fry with onion until cooked, but not brown. (You may partly boil the potatoes before dicing). Beat the eggs well and pour over cooked potatoes and onion (use large pan). When cooked on one side, turn it over. I slide it on to a plate and turn it over. Then serve flat on a plate and cut into sections.

serves 4

Potato Pie

1 lb potatoes
¼ lb butter melted
4 spring onions, chopped
    finely
2 tablespoons marjoram
    leaves
Salt and pepper to taste
Buttered breadcrumbs

Peel potatoes and slice very thinly. In a well-buttered casserole place a layer of potatoes, sprinkle with spring onions, marjoram leaves, salt and pepper, pour over half the butter, fill with rest of potatoes, pour over rest of butter and sprinkle buttered breadcrumbs on top. Cook in 350°F or no. 4 oven for 1 to 1¼ hours.

serves 3–4

Shepherd's Pie

2 cups mashed potatoes
2 cups cooked meat,
    finely chopped
½ cup celery, chopped
2 tablespoons parsley
2 eggs, separated
½ cup gravy
Salt
Paprika

Prepare the potatoes by the mashed potatoes recipe and beat in 2 egg yolks. Beat egg whites until stiff and fold into potatoes. Place 1 cup of the potatoes into well-buttered casserole.

Combine the meat, celery, parsley, gravy, salt and paprika and put over potatoes, place the other cup of potatoes on top and cook in 400°F or no. 6 oven for about 30 minutes.

serves 4

Cottage Pie

2 cups mashed potatoes
1 lb minced steak
1 onion, chopped finely
1 clove garlic, chopped
    finely
2 rashers of bacon,
    chopped finely
1 cup gravy
1 teaspoon mixed herbs
Salt and pepper to taste

Fry bacon, add garlic and onion, fry few minutes, add meat and cook for 5 minutes, browning a little, add gravy, herbs, salt and pepper and cook for 15 minutes. Place in casserole or oven-proof dish, top with mashed potatoes and bake in oven 350°F or no. 4 for 45 minutes.

serves 4

American Potato Kedgeree

2 cups cooked potatoes,
    diced
1 onion, chopped
2 cups cooked kidney
    beans
2 eggs, hard-boiled and
    chopped
¼ cup butter
1½ teaspoon curry
    powder
1 teaspoon lemon juice
Salt and pepper to taste

Fry onion in butter, add curry powder, lemon juice, salt and pepper and cook for 5 minutes, add potatoes, beans and eggs and heat all together.

serves 6

Castillian Potatoes

2 lb potatoes
1 large onion, chopped
1 clove garlic, chopped
   finely
1 tablespoon flour
1 small bay leaf, crumbled
½ cup oil
1 teaspoon paprika
Salt to taste

Peel and cut potatoes in thin slices, soak in cold water and dry well. Fry onion and garlic in oil; when they just begin to brown, add potatoes, bay leaf, paprika and salt, shake pan occasionally and when potatoes begin to soften, add flour and mix in, add just enough boiling water to cover potatoes, put lid on pan and simmer for 1 hour.

serves 6

Stewed Potatoes of Holland

2 cups raw potatoes,
diced
1 onion, sliced
1 teaspoon parsley,
   chopped
1½ cups boiling water
1 tablespoon butter
2 teaspoons flour
Salt and pepper to taste

Cook onion in butter for 5 minutes, add potatoes, parsley, salt and pepper and boiling water, cover and cook for 30 minutes. Add a little cold water to flour and stir to paste, add to potatoes and heat through.

serves 4

Pommes De Terre Ragout

8 medium potatoes
2 tablespoons butter
1 tablespoon flour
1 pint water
Bouquet garni
   (3 sprigs parsley
   1 sprig thyme
   1 bay leaf tied together)
Salt and pepper

Peel and slice potatoes in ½-inch slices. Melt butter and stir in flour, allow it to brown a little, add water gradually, stirring until smooth; add bouquet garni, salt and pepper and potatoes, simmer gently until potatoes are cooked, about 1 hour, make sure they do not burn. Remove bouquet garni, pour into serving dish.

serves 4

Spanish Potatoes with Garlic

2 lb potatoes
2 cloves garlic
1 bay leaf, crushed
1 slice bread
1 teaspoon saffron
6 almonds, ground
1 sprig parsley
½ cup oil
Salt and pepper to taste

Fry in oil, the slice of bread, garlic, bay leaf, parsley and almonds for 3 or 4 minutes, drain, save oil, add saffron to bread mixture and pound all to a paste. Peel and slice the potatoes thinly, mix with paste, add salt and pepper, put in casserole dish, pour remaining oil over all the potato mixture, cover and cook in 350°F or no. 4 oven for 1¼ hours.

serves 6

Desert Potato Mould

Potatoes, finely grated
   (about 5 medium size)
3 tablespoons fine sugar
   grated rind of 1 lemon
or
   1 orange
½ pint cream
2 eggs

Beat the eggs and sugar together until frothy, add grated rind of lemon or orange and cream, stir in enough grated potato to make a very thick batter; pour into a greased mould and bake in 350°F or no. 4 oven for 1 hour. Turn out on round plate and serve with lemon or orange sauce.

serves 4

Lemon or orange sauce
1 cup sugar
¼ cup butter
2 eggs, beaten
1 teaspoon lemon or
   orange rind
3 tablespoons lemon or
   orange juice
½ cup water

Cook all ingredients in top of double boiler, stirring until thick and smooth.

Potatoes De Luxe

2 potatoes
1 small onion
¼ green pepper
1 egg beaten
3 tablespoons butter
Salt and pepper to taste

Peel potatoes and grate, chop very finely onion and green pepper, mix together with egg, salt and pepper. Melt butter in frying pan add potato mixture and cook over low flame until browned, turn and brown on other side, about 5 to 6 minutes on each side.

serves 2

Potatoes O'Brien

6 potatoes, cooked and
  cubed
1 green pepper, chopped
1 onion, chopped
¾ cup cheese, grated
1 cup milk
2 tablespoons butter,
  melted
1 tablespoon flour
Salt to taste
Paprika
Dash of cayenne pepper
Breadcrumbs

Add green peppers, onion, cheese, flour, salt, paprika and cayenne to potatoes. Put in a well greased casserole and pour milk over all, then melted butter, sprinkle breadcrumbs on top and bake in 350°F or no. 4 oven for 20 minutes.

serves 4

Russian Potato Babka

2 lb potatoes
1 large onion, chopped
2 tablespoons butter
2 tablespoons flour
½ teaspoon baking
  powder
Salt and pepper to taste

Fry onion in 1 tablespoon of butter. Peel and grate potatoes and add to onion with flour, baking powder, salt and pepper and mix well together. Place in well buttered casserole and dot with 1 tablespoon butter, cover and bake in 375°F or no. 5 oven for 1 hour.

serves 6

Pommes De Terre En Souffle

2 cups mashed potatoes
3 eggs, separated
Salt and pepper to taste

Make the mashed potato of mashed potatoes recipe, beat egg yolks and add to potatoes with salt and pepper and mix well. Beat egg whites until stiff and fold into potato mixture, place in a well buttered casserole or oven-proof dish, put into 375°F or no. 5 oven for 20 minutes until golden brown.

serves 4

Spanish Potatoes

2 cups cooked potatoes,
  diced
2 tablespoons green
  peppers, chopped
2 tablespoons pimento,
  chopped
½ cup cooked ham,
  chopped
1 tablespoon onion,
  chopped finely
3 tablespoons oil
Salt to taste
½ teaspoon paprika

Fry onion, green peppers and pimento in oil until golden brown, add potatoes, ham, salt and paprika and cook slowly until thoroughly heated.

serves 4

Potatoes Dijon Souffle

2 cups mashed potatoes
¾ cup cheese grated
2 eggs, separated
Salt and pepper to taste

Beat egg yolks, add to potatoes with cheese and mash well together. Beat egg whites until stiff and fold into potato mixture. Put into well buttered casserole or oven-proof dish and bake in 350°F or no. 4 oven for 30 minutes.

serves 4

Potatoes Normandy

1 lb potatoes, sliced fine
1 onion, sliced fine
2 leeks, white part,
  thinly sliced
Chicken stock
1 oz butter
1 cup cream
4 thin bacon rashers
Salt and pepper to taste

Fry onion and leeks in butter for few minutes, add bacon rashers and fry a few minutes longer, then add potatoes, salt and pepper and enough stock just to cover potato mixture, cover and cook until potatoes are tender, about 20 minutes; add cream and just heat, do not boil, pour into serving dish and garnish with parsley.

serves 4

Norwegian Potato-Sardine Pudding

4 medium potatoes, thinly
   sliced
2 onions, thinly sliced
6 oz sardines
3 eggs, well beaten
1½ cups milk
3 tablespoons butter,
   melted
Salt and pepper to taste

In a buttered caserole place a layer of potatoes, then sliced onions, then some sardines, repeat layers, finishing with layer of potatoes. Place 4 sardines, tail to middle on top of potatoes. Add milk to eggs with salt and pepper and pour into casserole. Cover and cook in 350°F or no. 4 oven for 1 hour.

serves 4

Conversions

For the American reader please note that
1 US = 16 fl oz
1 UK pint = 20 fl oz
1 US tablespoon holds 3 teaspoons or
                    1 large dessertspoon

Metric equivalents
¼ pint = 142 millilitres
½ pint = 283 millilitres
1 pint = 586 millilitres

1 oz =   28 grammes
2 oz =   56 grammes
3 oz =   85 grammes
4 oz = 113 grammes
7 oz = 198 grammes
8 oz = 226 grammes

½ lb (8 oz) = 226 grammes
1 lb   = 454 grammes
1½ lb = 672 grammes
2 lb   = 906 grammes

¾ in. =   6 mm
½ in. =   12 mm
¾ in. =   19 mm
1 in. =   25 mm
1½ in. =   38 mm
2 in. =   50 mm
2½ in. =   63 mm
3 in. =   76 mm
7 in. = 178 mm

300°F = 148°C
350°F = 176°C
375°F = 190°C
380°F = 193°C
395°F = 201°C
400°F = 204°C
425°F = 218°C